IS PUBLISHING

No nonsense Multiplication & Division

Ages 9–10 **Book 3**

Jackie Andrews • Jude Callaghan • Suzi de Gouveia

Title: No Nonsense Multiplication & Division Ages 9-10 Book 3

Authors: Suzi de Gouveia, Jackie Andrews and Jude Callaghan

Editor: Tanya Tremewan

Book code: PB00083

ISBN: 978-1-908735-63-8

Published: 2012

Publisher: TTS Group Ltd

Park Lane Business Park
Kirkby-in-Ashfield
Notts, NG17 9GU
Tel: 0800 318 686
Fax: 0800 137 525

Website: www.tts-shopping.com

About the authors: Suzi is the enthusiastic headteacher of St Teresa's Primary School in Christchurch, New Zealand. She has international teaching experience and has had the pleasure of teaching in a multi-cultural environment. Over 20 years of teaching have enabled Suzi to develop a wealth of ideas and resources to best help children in their learning.

Jackie is an experienced teacher who has taught primary school children in both New Zealand and the United Kingdom. As a mother of four young children she is beginning to wonder where the time to diversify has gone.

Jude is an experienced, enthusiastic teacher with a passion for teaching and learning. Her teaching programmes are innovative and exciting. She has joined the writing team to share her deep understanding and wealth of ideas.

Contents

Introduction

This book has been designed to support teaching and learning in mathematics in Year 5.

This book contains two sections. The first section comprises **activity sheets** to support the learning and consolidation of concepts in the curriculum (see links below).

Number knowledge concepts covered are:

- recall groups of two, three, five and ten in numbers to 100
- recall groups of 10 and 100 that can be made from a four-digit number
- record the results of mental calculations using multiplication and division equations and diagrams
- recall all the basic multiplication facts.

The strategies covered in this book are:

- solve multiplication and division problems from other known facts, using a variety of strategies, including doubling, adding and subtracting, reversing and rounding
- multiply by tens, hundreds and thousands
- change the order of factors to make a multiplication problem easier
- solve division problems using equal sharing and find the number of equivalent sets.

A number of word problems in this book reinforce the common types of context for multiplication and division (equal groups, rate, comparison, part–whole, cartesian product and rectangular area).

The second section is comprised of **activity cards**. These templates can be used in a variety of ways to develop number knowledge through independent, individual and group work.

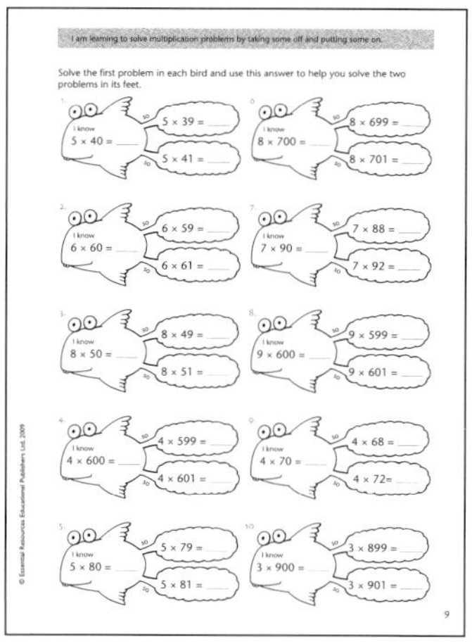

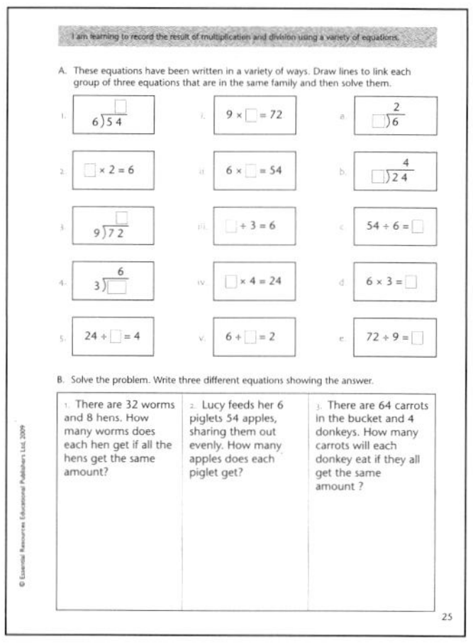

Curriculum links

Strand	Objectives *Most children learn to:*
Year 5	
Counting and understanding number	• count from any given number in whole-number steps; relate the numbers to their position on a number line • explain what each digit represents in whole numbers
Knowing and using number facts	• recall quickly multiplication facts up to 10 × 10; derive quickly corresponding division facts • identify pairs of factors of two-digit whole numbers • use knowledge of place value, number facts and inverse operations to estimate and check calculations

Source: Adapted from Primary Framework for Literacy and Mathematics, 2006

Working with place value in whole numbers (Part 1)

I am learning how many tens and hundreds are in a whole number.

A. Show the answer on the number fans.

1. How many tens are in 6,745?

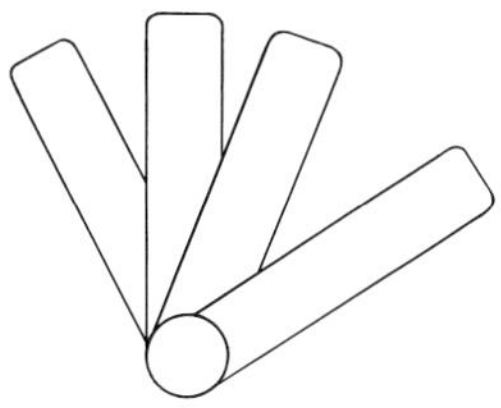

2. How many tens are in 45,678?

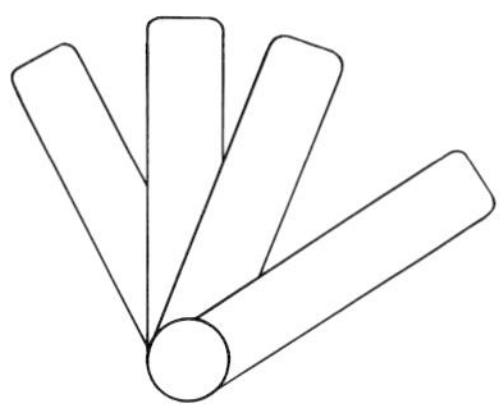

3. How many hundreds are in 2,879?

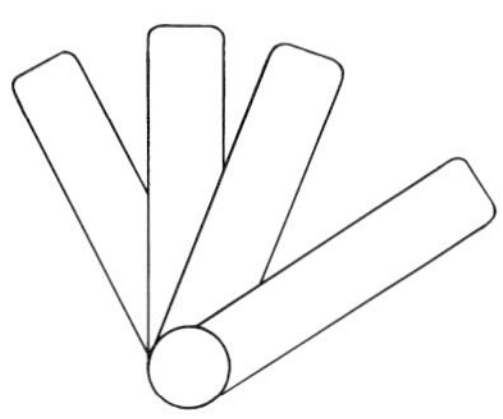

4. How many tens are in 64,321?

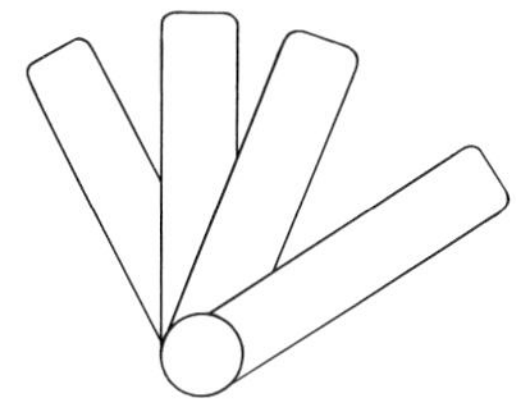

5. How many hundreds are in 59,704?

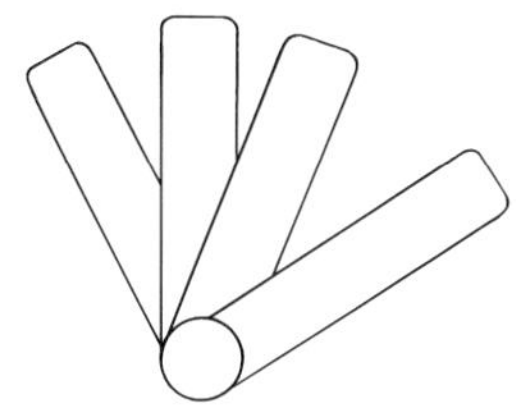

6. How many hundreds are in 9,845?

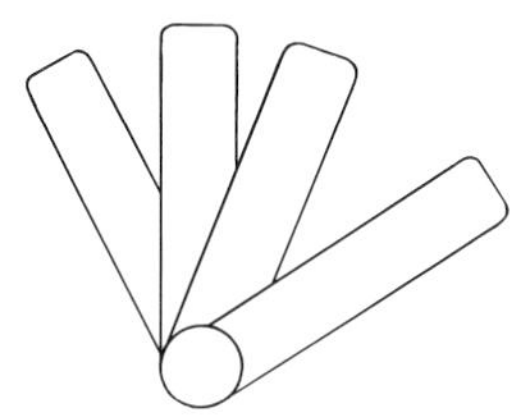

B. How many hundreds are coming out of the first number machine? How many tens are coming out of the second number machine? Complete the number machines to find out.

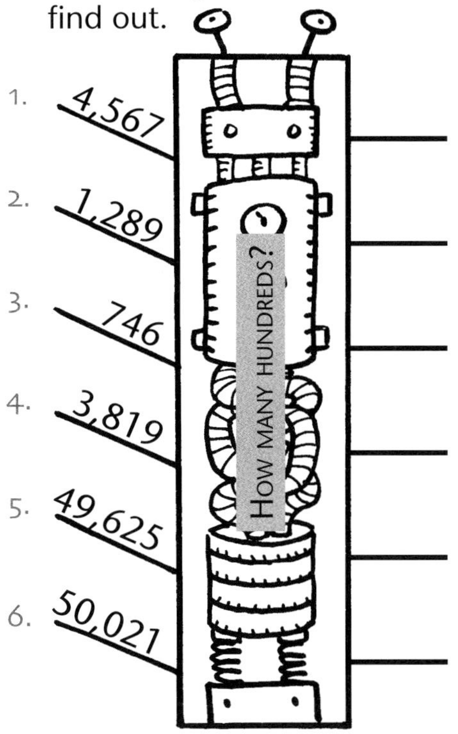

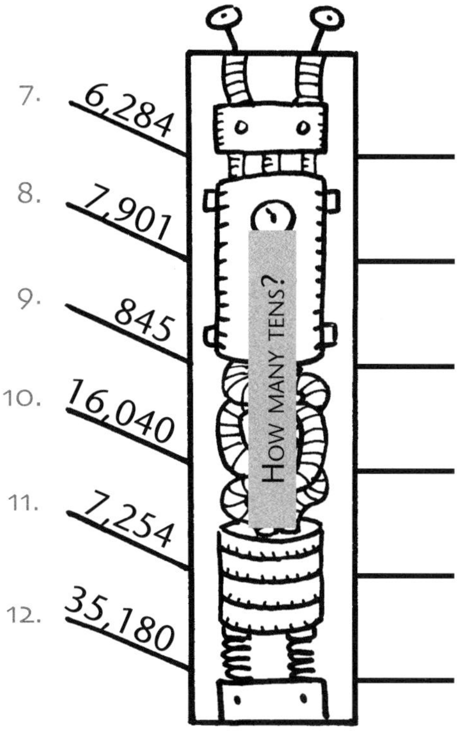

I am learning how many ones, tens, hundreds and thousands are in a whole number.

How much money has each piggy bank got in total? Use spare paper for working space.

1. 4 £100 notes
63 £10 notes
25 £1 coins

2. 2 £1,000 notes
13 £100 notes
37 £10 notes
6 £1 coins

3. 45 £100 notes
3 £10 notes
26 £1 coins

4. 18 £100 notes
35 £10 notes
76 £1 coins

5. 23 £1,000 notes
17 £10 notes
28 £1 coins

6. 4 £1,000 notes
36 £100 notes
27 £1 coins

7. 11 £100 notes
26 £10 notes
15 £1 coins

8. 9 £1,000 notes
14 £100 notes
21 £10 notes
11 £1 coins

9. 26 £100 notes
123 £1 coins

10. 14 £100 notes
27 £10 notes
106 £1 coins

I am learning how many ones, tens, hundreds and thousands are in a whole number.

Find out how much money each twin has. Underline the one that has more.

	Twin 1	Twin 2
1.	14 £100 notes 76 £1 coins	10 £100 notes 45 £10 notes 6 £1 coins
2.	69 £10 notes 46 £1 coins	7 £100 notes 2 £10 notes 6 £1 coins
3.	49 £100 notes 115 £1 coins	49 £100 notes 80 £10 notes 45 £1 coins
4.	3 £1,000 notes 23 £100 notes 143 £1 coins	5 £1,000 notes 42 £10 notes 33 £1 coins
5.	6 £100 notes 17 £10 notes 46 £1 coins	5 £100 notes 23 £10 notes 66 £1 coins
6.	24 £100 notes 36 £10 notes 18 £1 coins	2 £1,000 notes 38 £10 notes 28 £1 coins
7.	9 £100 notes 7 £10 notes 37 £1 coins	6 £100 notes 48 £10 notes 65 £1 coins

Multiplying by taking some off and putting some on

I am learning to solve multiplication problems by taking some off and putting some on.

Complete the first problem in each bird and use this answer to help you complete the two problems in its feet.

1\. I know 5 × 30 = ______
so 5 × 29 = ______
so 5 × 31 = ______

2\. I know 6 × 40 = ______
so 6 × 39 = ______
so 6 × 41 = ______

3\. I know 8 × 30 = ______
so 8 × 29 = ______
so 8 × 31 = ______

4\. I know 4 × 200 = ______
so 4 × 199 = ______
so 4 × 201 = ______

5\. I know 5 × 90 = ______
so 5 × 89 = ______
so 5 × 91 = ______

6\. I know 8 × 800 = ______
so 8 × 799 = ______
so 8 × 801 = ______

7\. I know 7 × 70 = ______
so 7 × 68 = ______
so 7 × 72 = ______

8\. I know 9 × 300 = ______
so 9 × 299 = ______
so 9 × 301 = ______

9\. I know 4 × 50 = ______
so 4 × 48 = ______
so 4 × 52= ______

10\. I know 3 × 700 = ______
so 3 × 699 = ______
so 3 × 701 = ______

I am learning to solve multiplication problems by taking some off and putting some on.

Complete the first problem in each bird and use this answer to help you complete the two problems in its feet.

1. I know 5 × 40 = ______
   so 5 × 39 = ______
   so 5 × 41 = ______

2. I know 6 × 60 = ______
   so 6 × 59 = ______
   so 6 × 61 = ______

3. I know 8 × 50 = ______
   so 8 × 49 = ______
   so 8 × 51 = ______

4. I know 4 × 600 = ______
   so 4 × 599 = ______
   so 4 × 601 = ______

5. I know 5 × 80 = ______
   so 5 × 79 = ______
   so 5 × 81 = ______

6. I know 8 × 700 = ______
   so 8 × 699 = ______
   so 8 × 701 = ______

7. I know 7 × 90 = ______
   so 7 × 88 = ______
   so 7 × 92 = ______

8. I know 9 × 600 = ______
   so 9 × 599 = ______
   so 9 × 601 = ______

9. I know 4 × 70 = ______
   so 4 × 68 = ______
   so 4 × 72= ______

10. I know 3 × 900 = ______
    so 3 × 899 = ______
    so 3 × 901 = ______

I am learning to solve multiplication problems by taking some off and putting some on.

Multiply the numbers in the white boxes with the shaded number at the start of the same row. Record your answers on the blank grid below.

91 ×	7	4	6	9
49 ×	5	8	7	4
31 ×	3	5	2	9
69 ×	8	2	6	4
21 ×	7	6	9	3

I am learning to solve multiplication problems by taking some off and putting some on.

Multiply the numbers in the white boxes with the shaded number at the start of the same row. Record your answers on the blank grid below.

9 ×	22 tens	18 ones	19 tens	21 ones
6 ×	31 tens	49 ones	51 tens	28 ones
8 ×	52 tens	69 ones	39 tens	58 ones
4 ×	41 tens	59 ones	32 tens	68 ones
7 ×	29 tens	38 ones	48 tens	42 ones

I am learning to solve multiplication problems by taking some off and putting some on.

Theo has just got a job as Head Zoo Keeper at Timbucktoo Zoo. Help him solve these problems.

1. It takes 5 minutes to feed a lion. How many minutes will it take to feed 19 lions?

2. It takes 18 minutes to feed 1 elephant. How many minutes will it take to feed 7 elephants?

3. It takes 22 minutes to feed 1 crocodile. How many minutes will it take to feed 9 crocodiles?

4. It takes 4 minutes to immunise a monkey. How many minutes will it take to immunise 32 monkeys?

5. Theo can clean out one rabbit cage in 7 minutes. How many minutes will it take to clean out 59 cages?

6. It takes 59 minutes to groom a camel. How many minutes will it take to groom 2 camels?

7. He can brush one llama in 6 minutes. How long will it take to brush 49 llamas?

8. It takes 79 minutes to wash 1 rhino. How many minutes will it take to wash 6 rhinos?

9. It takes 5 minutes to check 1 zebra's hooves. How many minutes will it take to check the hooves of 19 zebras?

I am learning to solve multiplication problems by taking some off and putting some on.

Wilber, Winston and Toby are training for the Olympic swim team. Help them solve these problems.

1. On Monday Wilber swam 7 times as many lengths as Toby. Toby swam 11 lengths. How many lengths did Wilber swim?

2. Winston swam 9 times as many lengths as Toby. Toby swam 11 lengths. How many lengths did Winston swim?

3. On Tuesday Winston swam 7 times as many lengths as Toby. Toby swam 31 lengths. How many lengths did Winston swim?

4. Wilber swam 6 times as many lengths as Toby. Toby swam 31 lengths. How many lengths did Wilber swim?

5. On Wednesday Toby swam 9 times as many lengths as Wilber. Wilber swam 19 lengths. How many lengths did Toby swim?

6. Winston swam 7 times as many lengths as Wilber. Wilber swam 19 lengths. How many lengths did Winston swim?

7. On Thursday Winston swam 7 times as many lengths as Toby. Toby swam 22 lengths. How many lengths did Winston swim?

8. Wilber swam 9 times as many lengths as Toby. Toby swam 22 lengths. How many lengths did Wilber swim?

9. On Friday Toby and Wilber both swam 3 times as many lengths as Winston. Winston swam 29 lengths. How many lengths did Toby and Wilber each swim?

I am learning to solve multiplication problems by taking some off and putting some on.

Theo has just got a job as Head Zoo Keeper at Timbucktoo Zoo. Help him solve these problems so that he can feed the animals.

Zoo food	Working
1. 1 elephant eats 29 bales of hay each week. How many bales of hay would 8 elephants eat?	
2. 1 lion eats 19 kilograms of meat each week. How many kilograms of meat would 6 lions eat?	
3. 1 monkey eats 198 nuts a month. How many nuts do 8 monkeys eat?	
4. A panda bear eats 18 kilograms of bamboo each month. How many kilograms of bamboo would 7 pandas eat?	
5. A blue tooth lizard can eat 62 flies in a week. How many flies would 7 blue tooth lizards eat?	
6. 3 camels eat 29 bales of hay altogether each week. How many bales of hay would 9 camels eat?	
7. The giant python eats 19 mice each month. How many mice would he eat in a year?	

Solving sharing division problems

I am learning to solve sharing division problems by using multiplication facts.

These children love to eat sweets. Solve each problem to find out how many sweets a child has or how long their sweets will last.

Problem	Working
1. Maria has 4 times as many sweets as Max. Maria has 28 sweets. How many does Max have?	
2. Henry has 6 times as many sweets as Max. Henry has 42 sweets. How many sweets does Max have?	
3. Glenn can eat 5 lollipops in 20 minutes. How many minutes does it take him to eat 1 lollipop?	
4. Max has 7 times more marshmallows than Glenn. Max has 49 marshmallow. How many marshmallows does Glenn have?	
5. Maria and her friends eat 6 packets of sweets in 54 minutes. How many minutes does it take them to eat 1 packet of sweets?	
6. Maria has 5 boxes of chocolates. There are 45 chocolates altogether. How many chocolates are in each box?	
7. Glenn has 3 times more sweets than Maria. Maria has 54 sweets. How many sweets does Glenn have?	

I am learning to solve sharing division problems by using multiplication and division.

Fiona and her friends collect stickers. Solve each problem to find out how many stickers a girl has or how much the stickers cost.

Problem	Working
1. Fiona can fit 63 stickers evenly on 9 pages of her album. How many stickers are on each page?	
2. Rebecca has 4 times as many "glow in the dark" stickers as Fiona. Rebecca has 36 stickers. How many does Fiona have?	
3. Fiona has 3 times as many sparkly stickers as Amrit. Fiona has 18 sparkly stickers. How many does Amrit have?	
4. Amrit can buy 4 special stickers for 80 pence. How much does each special sticker cost?	
5. Rebecca fits 56 stickers evenly on 7 pages. How many stickers does she have on each page?	
6. Fiona buys 5 special stickers for 90 pence. How much does each special sticker cost?	
7. Amrit has 7 times as many "happy face" stickers as Rebecca. Amrit has 28 "happy face" stickers. How many does Rebecca have?	

Working with place value in whole numbers (Part 2)

I am learning to solve "how many equal sets of" problems by reversing multiplication facts.

How much do you know about packing fruit and vegetables and how quickly you can eat one? Solve these problems to help you find out.

Problem	Working
1. How many apples can you eat in 24 minutes if it takes 4 minutes to eat 1 apple?	
2. 4 apples fit into each box. If 36 apples must be packed, how many boxes are needed?	
3. How many oranges can be peeled in 18 minutes if it takes 2 minutes to peel 1 orange?	
4. The delivery truck has 27 boxes of apples and 3 boxes of bananas. How many times more boxes of apples are there than boxes of bananas?	
5. How many bananas can you eat in 28 minutes if it takes you 4 minutes to eat 1 banana?	
6. How many boxes of oranges can be packed in 48 minutes if it takes 6 minutes to pack 1 box?	
7. How many potatoes can be peeled in 42 minutes if it takes 3 minutes to peel 1 potato?	

I am learning to solve multiplication and division problems.

Gracie, Caitlin and Brooke all played netball on Saturday morning. Help them solve these problems to see how they are doing.

Problem	Working
1. In their first game each of the three girls scored 6 goals. How many goals did they score altogether?	
2. Gracie can score one goal every 6 minutes. How long will it take her to score 7 goals?	
3. Caitlin scored 4 times as many goals as Brooke. Brooke scored 56 goals. How many goals did Caitlin score?	
4. In their second game each of the three girls scored 9 goals. How many goals did they score altogether?	
5. Caitlin can score one goal every 4 minutes. How many minutes will it take her to score 20 goals?	
6. Gracie scored 7 times as many goals as Caitlin. Caitlin scored 49 goals. How many goals did Gracie score?	
7. In their third game Brooke scored 3 times as many goals as Gracie. Gracie scored 9 goals. How many goals did Brooke score?	

I am learning to solve multiplication and division problems.

Gracie, Caitlin and Brooke all played netball on Saturday morning. Help them solve these problems to see how they are doing.

Problem	Working
1. In the end of season tournament the three girls scored 24 goals each. How many goals did they score altogether?	
2. For their first game the three girls scored an equal number of goals. They scored 24 goals altogether. How many did each girl score?	
3. Caitlin scored 7 times as many goals as Brooke. Brooke scored 8 goals. How many goals did Caitlin score?	
4. Gracie scored 8 goals in 64 minutes. How long did it take to score 1 goal?	
5. For their second game the three girls scored an equal number of goals. They scored 51 goals altogether. How many did each girl score?	
6. Caitlin scored 4 goals in 20 minutes. How long did it take to score 1 goal?	

Doubling to work out times facts

I am learning to use doubling to work out my times facts.

Complete the first times tables problem in each box and use this answer to help you complete the second one.

1.
$2 \times 8 =$ ____
double ↓ double ↓
$4 \times 8 =$ ____

2.
$2 \times 9 =$ ____
double ↓ double ↓
$4 \times 9 =$ ____

3.
$4 \times 4 =$ ____
double ↓ double ↓
$8 \times 4 =$ ____

4.
$2 \times 6 =$ ____
double ↓ double ↓
$4 \times 6 =$ ____

5.
$4 \times 7 =$ ____
double ↓ double ↓
$8 \times 7 =$ ____

6.
$4 \times 3 =$ ____
double ↓ double ↓
$8 \times 3 =$ ____

7.
$4 \times 5 =$ ____
double ↓ double ↓
$8 \times 5 =$ ____

8.
$2 \times 5 =$ ____
double ↓ double ↓
$4 \times 5 =$ ____

9.
$2 \times 7 =$ ____
double ↓ double ↓
$4 \times 7 =$ ____

10.
$2 \times 25 =$ ____
double ↓ double ↓
$4 \times 25 =$ ____

I am learning to use doubling to work out my times facts.

Complete the first times tables problem in each box and use this answer to help you complete the second one.

1.

$3 \times 5 =$ ____

double ↓ double ↓

$6 \times 5 =$ ____

2.

$3 \times 8 =$ ____

double ↓ double ↓

$6 \times 8 =$ ____

3.

$3 \times 6 =$ ____

double ↓ double ↓

$6 \times 6 =$ ____

4.

$3 \times 2 =$ ____

double ↓ double ↓

$6 \times 2 =$ ____

5.

$4 \times 6 =$ ____

double ↓ double ↓

$8 \times 6 =$ ____

6.

$3 \times 9 =$ ____

double ↓ double ↓

$6 \times 9 =$ ____

7.

$3 \times 4 =$ ____

double ↓ double ↓

$6 \times 4 =$ ____

8.

$3 \times 7 =$ ____

double ↓ double ↓

$6 \times 7 =$ ____

9.

$3 \times 3 =$ ____

double ↓ double ↓

$6 \times 3 =$ ____

10.

$4 \times 8 =$ ____

double ↓ double ↓

$8 \times 8 =$ ____

Using multiplication and division problems to determine the number of sets

I am learning to solve "how many sets of" using multiplication and division problems.

Count to find how many rows are in each problem. Write how many rows you have counted so far in the circle at the end of each row. Then finish the problem.

1.

1	2	3	1
4	5	6	
7	8	9	
10	11	12	
13	14	15	
16	17	18	

$3\overline{)18}$ □

18 ÷ 3 = □

2.

1	2	3	4	1
5	6	7	8	
9	10	11	12	
13	14	15	16	
17	18	19	20	
21	22	23	24	

$4\overline{)24}$ □

24 ÷ 4 = □

3.

1	2	3	4	5	6	1
7	8	9	10	11	12	
13	14	15	16	17	18	
19	20	21	22	23	24	
25	26	27	28	29	30	
31	32	33	34	35	36	
37	38	39	40	41	42	

$6\overline{)42}$ □

42 ÷ 6 = □

4.

1	2	3	4	5	6	7	1
8	9	10	11	12	13	14	
15	16	17	18	19	20	21	
22	23	24	25	26	27	28	

$7\overline{)28}$ □

28 ÷ 7 = □

5.

1	2	3	4	5	6	1
7	8	9	10	11	12	
13	14	15	16	17	18	
19	20	21	22	23	24	

$6\overline{)24}$ □

24 ÷ 6 = □

6.

1	2	3	4	1
5	6	7	8	
9	10	11	12	
13	14	15	16	
17	18	19	20	
21	22	23	24	
25	26	27	28	
29	30	31	32	
33	34	35	36	

$4\overline{)36}$ □

36 ÷ 4 = □

I am learning to solve "how many sets of" using multiplication and division problems.

Count to find how many rows are in each problem. Write how many rows you have counted so far in the circle at the end of each row. Then finish the problem.

1.

1	2	3	4	5	6	1
7	8	9	10	11	12	
13	14	15	16	17	18	
19	20	21	22	23	24	
25	26	27	28	29	30	

6)30 □

30 ÷ 6 = □

2.

1	2	3	4	5	6	7	1
8	9	10	11	12	13	14	
15	16	17	18	19	20	21	

7)21 □

21 ÷ 7 = □

3.

1	2	3	4	5	6	7	1
8	9	10	11	12	13	14	
15	16	17	18	19	20	21	
22	23	24	25	26	27	28	
29	30	31	32	33	34	35	
36	37	38	39	40	41	42	

7)42 □

42 ÷ 7 = □

4.

1	2	3	4	5	6	7	8	9	1
10	11	12	13	14	15	16	17	18	
19	20	21	22	23	24	25	26	27	
28	29	30	31	32	33	34	35	36	

9)36 □

36 ÷ 9 = □

5.

1	2	3	4	1
5	6	7	8	
9	10	11	12	
13	14	15	16	
17	18	19	20	
21	22	23	24	
25	26	27	28	

4)28 □

28 ÷ 4 = □

6.

1	2	3	1
4	5	6	
7	8	9	
10	11	12	
13	14	15	
16	17	18	
19	20	21	
22	23	24	

3)24 □

24 ÷ 3 = □

Recording answers with a variety of equations

I am learning to record the result of multiplication and division using a variety of equations.

A. These equations have been written in a variety of ways. Draw lines to link each group of three equations that are in the same family and then complete them.

1.	$\begin{array}{r}\square\\ 6\overline{)42}\end{array}$	i.	$7 \times 5 = \square$	a.	$9 \times 7 = \square$
2.	$32 \div \square = 8$	ii.	$27 \div 3 = \square$	b.	$\square \times 8 = 32$
3.	$\square \div 9 = 7$	iii.	$42 \div 6 = \square$	c.	$\square \div 5 = 7$
4.	$\begin{array}{r}\square\\ 3\overline{)27}\end{array}$	iv.	$\begin{array}{r}8\\ \square\overline{)32}\end{array}$	d.	$3 \times \square = 27$
5.	$\begin{array}{r}7\\ 5\overline{)\square}\end{array}$	v.	$\begin{array}{r}7\\ 9\overline{)\square}\end{array}$	e.	$6 \times \square = 42$

B. Complete the problem. Write three different equations showing the answer.

1. Mary and her 5 friends eat 36 strawberries. How many strawberries does each person eat?	2. Robert and his 8 friends make 36 biscuits and share them out evenly to give away to their grandmas. How many biscuits does each person give away?	3. There are 18 sweets in the jar. Each child gets 3 sweets. How many children are there altogether?

I am learning to record the result of multiplication and division using a variety of equations.

A. These equations have been written in a variety of ways. Draw lines to link each group of three equations that are in the same family and then complete them.

1. $\begin{array}{r}\square\\6\overline{)54}\end{array}$	i. $9 \times \square = 72$	a. $\begin{array}{r}2\\\square\overline{)6}\end{array}$
2. $\square \times 2 = 6$	ii. $6 \times \square = 54$	b. $\begin{array}{r}4\\\square\overline{)24}\end{array}$
3. $\begin{array}{r}\square\\9\overline{)72}\end{array}$	iii. $\square \div 3 = 6$	c. $54 \div 6 = \square$
4. $\begin{array}{r}6\\3\overline{)\square}\end{array}$	iv. $\square \times 4 = 24$	d. $6 \times 3 = \square$
5. $24 \div \square = 4$	v. $6 \div \square = 2$	e. $72 \div 9 = \square$

B. Complete the problem. Write three different equations showing the answer.

1. There are 32 worms and 8 hens. How many worms does each hen get if all the hens get the same amount?	2. Lucy feeds her 6 piglets 54 apples, sharing them out evenly. How many apples does each piglet get?	3. There are 64 carrots in the bucket and 4 donkeys. How many carrots will each donkey eat if they all get the same amount ?

Combining multiplication, division, addition and subtraction strategies

I am learning to solve problems using a combination of multiplication, division, addition and subtraction strategies.

Park School is going to buy new uniforms for its sports teams. Help the school to work out how much each set of uniforms will cost.

Problem	Working
1. Netball: 8 skirts £49 each 8 tops £21 each 8 bibs £28 each	
2. Rugby: 20 jerseys £62 each 20 shorts £58 each 20 pairs of socks £19 a pair	
3. Football: 12 tops £70 each 12 shorts £40 each 12 pairs of socks £20 a pair	
4. Hockey: 9 tops £60 each 9 shorts £49 each 9 pairs of socks £19 a pair	

I am learning to solve problems using a combination of multiplication, division, addition and subtraction strategies.

Use the strategies that you know for multiplication, division, addition and subtraction to help you solve these problems.

Problem	Working
1. Matthew gets £90 for his birthday. He buys 2 CDs for £29 each, a book for £15 and 2 bags of sweets for £2.50 each. How much change does he have?	
2. Rishi is having a birthday party with 7 of his friends. At the party they eat 4 pizzas that cost £15 each and 4 large bottles of fizzy drink that cost £2 each. Each has a portion of chips at £2.50 each and they watch 3 DVDs at £8 each. How much does it cost for each person at the party? What is the total cost?	
3. Natalie and her 6 friends go to the cinema at £8 per person. Each person has a box of popcorn at £5.50, a large drink at £4 and a packet of sweets at £2.50. How much does each person spend? How much does it cost altogether?	

I am learning to solve problems using a combination of multiplication, division, addition and subtraction strategies.

Use the strategies that you know for multiplication, division, addition and subtraction to help you solve these problems.

Problem	Working
1. Sam and his friends sell sausages at school to raise money for some new basketball tops. Each sausage costs £2. How much money do they get from each class if all the children order a sausage? Class 1 has 29 children. Class 2 has 35 children. Class 3 has 19 children. Class 4 has 21 children. The fundraisers have to pay £6 for bread, £15 for the sausages and £3 for tomato sauce. How much profit have they made? The tops are going to cost £350 in total. How much more money do they have to raise?	
2. The 29 children in Class 7 have raised £750 towards their class camp. If the camp is going to cost each child £30, have they raised enough money already? If not, how much more money does the class have to raise?	

I am learning to solve problems using a combination of multiplication, division, addition and subtraction strategies.

Use the strategies that you know for multiplication, division, addition and subtraction to help you solve these problems.

Problem	Working
1. Ben sells 3 times as many newspapers as Matt. If Matt sells 58 newspapers, how many does Ben sell? How many newspapers do the two boys sell altogether?	
2. Molly, Ruby, Harry and Tom earn £84 altogether from cleaning windows. They have to pay £12 for buckets, cloths and window cleaning liquid. If they share the rest of the money evenly, how much money does each person get?	
3. Sabin and two of his friends earn £75 a month altogether from doing a paper round. If they share the money equally, how much money does each child get? How much does each child earn in a year?	

Easy peasy (pages 33–35)

Aim: To encourage the children to multiply the easy numbers first.

To **make**:

- copy the number cards and multiplication boards onto coloured paper
- laminate and cut up the cards
- store them in a ziplock bag.

To **play**:

- place the number cards face down in a pile
- each child has their own multiplication board
- the first child takes one of the number cards and places it face up for everyone to see
- with the ultimate goal of multiplying all three numbers together, the children first multiply the two easiest numbers on the card together then record their answer on their multiplication board with a whiteboard pen and complete the equation with the third number
- the first child finished is the winner of that round.

2 × 5 = 10

10	×	3	=	30

Monster snap (pages 36–37)

Aim: To realise that different pairs of factors can have the same answer.

To **make**:

- copy the number cards onto coloured paper
- laminate and cut up the cards
- store them in a ziplock bag.

To **play**:

- deal the cards so that each child has the same amount, which they hold face down in a small pile
- in turn, each child places one of their cards in the middle face up, gradually forming a pile
- if the child puts a card that is either the answer to the card immediately underneath it or that has the same answer as that card, all the children race to be first to "snap" the pile
- the last child to run out of cards is the winner.

Multiplication race (page 38)

Aim: To reinforce the multiplying of tens, hundreds and thousands.

To **make**:

- copy the game board onto coloured paper
- laminate the game board
- create a place value dice by constructing a blank dice and writing the numbers 10, 100 and 1,000 on its six sides (ie, each number appears on two sides)
- store the game board, the place value dice and a normal dice in a ziplock bag.

To **play**:

- the first child rolls a normal dice and moves the number shown along the spaces on the game board
- the first child rolls the place value dice and multiplies the number that they have landed on by the number that they roll

  (eg, 497 × 10 or 497 × 100 or 497 × 1,000)
- other players confirm a correct answer or use a calculator to do so
- each time a child gets a correct answer, they score a point
- children take turns in this way until all players reach home
- the child who has the most points when they reach home is the winner.

Get in line (pages 39–41)

Aim: To reinforce the use of number lines to help solve division problems.

To **make**:

- copy the number lines and division equation cards onto coloured paper (note that you make the 1–36 number line by sticking together the number line to 18 and the number line from 19)
- laminate and cut up the cards
- store them in a ziplock bag.

To **play**:

- place the division cards face down in a pile
- each child takes a division card and then chooses the appropriate number line to show the equation
- using a whiteboard pen, they mark the solution to the problem at the correct place on the number line.

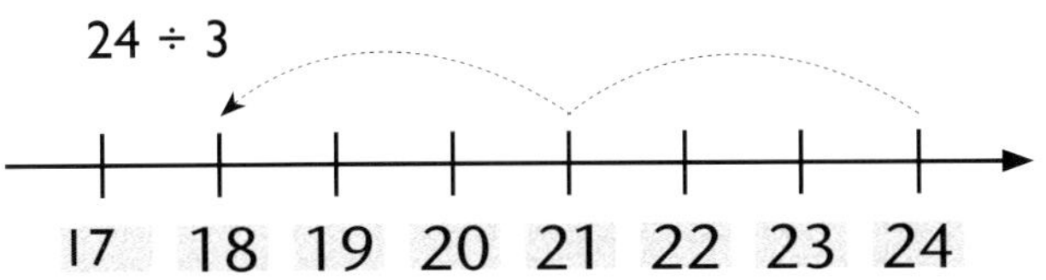

Fishy insides (pages 42–44)

Aim: To use the five times table to help solve problems.

To **make**:

- copy the large fish and multiplication equation cards onto coloured paper
- laminate and cut up the cards
- store them in a ziplock bag.

To **play**:

- place a multiplication equation card in the mouth of the fish
- using a whiteboard pen, solve the problem in the spaces provided inside the fish, writing the answer in the tail (see diagram on right).

Bingo (pages 45–46)

Aim: To recognise different pairs of factors that have the same answer.

To **make**:

- copy the bingo boards and multiplication cards onto coloured paper
- laminate the boards and cards and cut them out
- store them in a ziplock bag.

To **play**:

- each child has their own game board (four numbers), while the multiplication cards sit face down in a pile in the middle
- in turn, each child picks up a multiplication card and turns it over
- each child who has the answer to the multiplication card on their board writes the equation on their game board
- the winner is the first child to complete the board by writing two pairs of factors for each answer.

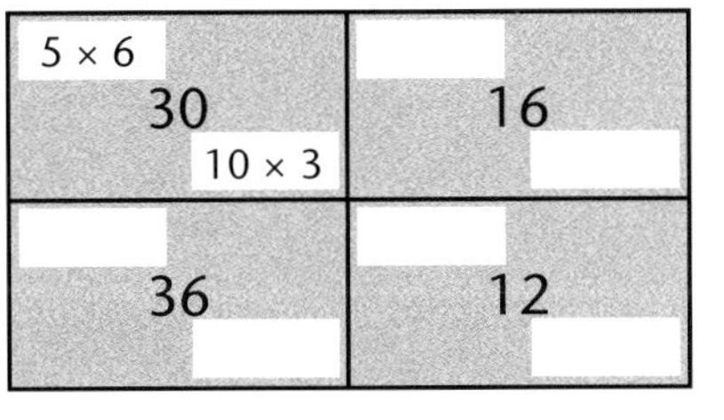

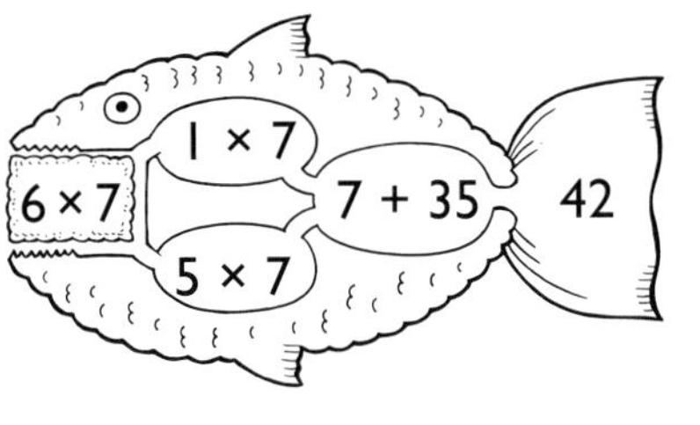

Links (pages 47–54)

Aim: To reinforce the multiplication facts.

To **make**:

- copy the links cards onto coloured paper (a different colour for each set)
- laminate the cards and cut them out
- store each set in a separate ziplock bag.

To **play** (either individually or in a group):

- choose a set of links cards
- players deal them out equally and look at their cards
- the child with the white star starts off by placing the card face up in the middle
- the child with the card that includes the answer to it (on the left) places this card on the left of the first card
- the game continues in this way
- the winner is the child who gets rid of all their cards first, or the game is completed when the black star is placed down.

Note: This is a good game to send home for families to play together.

Shady problems (page 55)

Aim: To reinforce multiplication problems that involve taking some off and putting some on.

To **make**:

- copy the number grids onto coloured paper
- fill in appropriate numbers on the top grid either before laminating (for a permanent number range) or after laminating (using a whiteboard pen for erasable numbers)
- store in a ziplock bag.

To **play** (individually):

- for each row of the top grid, the child multiplies the number in the shaded column by each other number in the row and records the answer with a whiteboard pen on the bottom grid.

Easy peasy

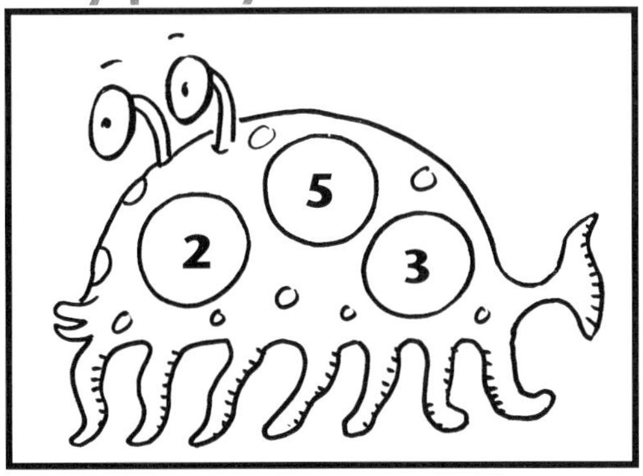

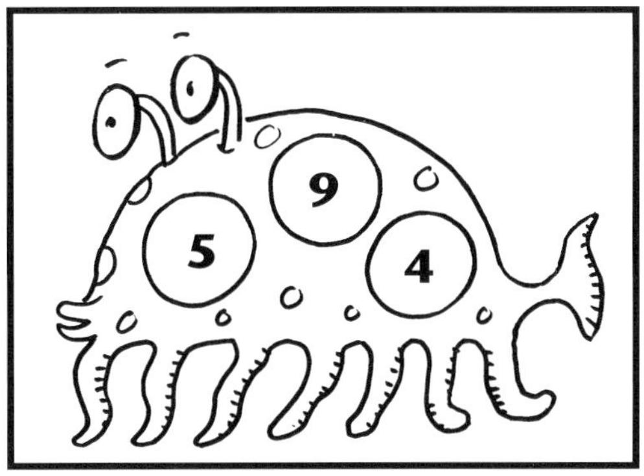

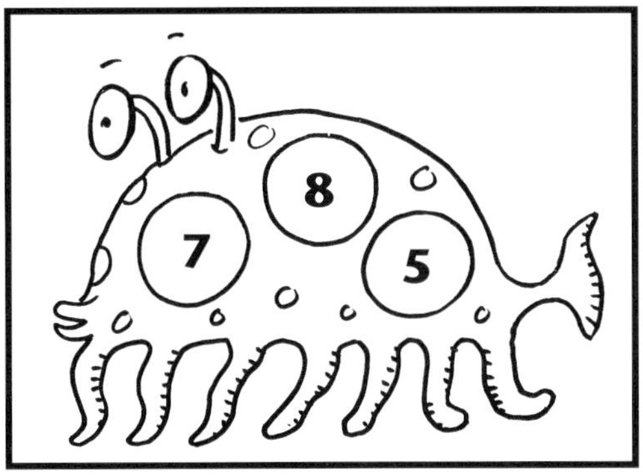

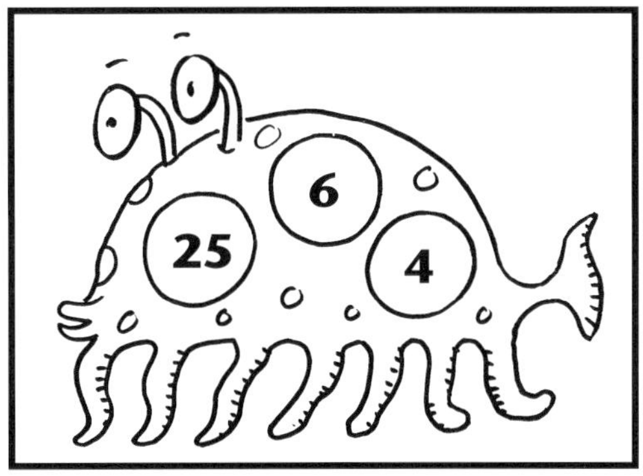

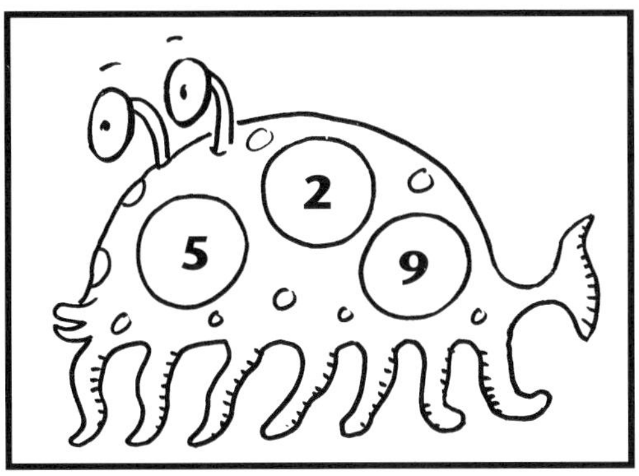

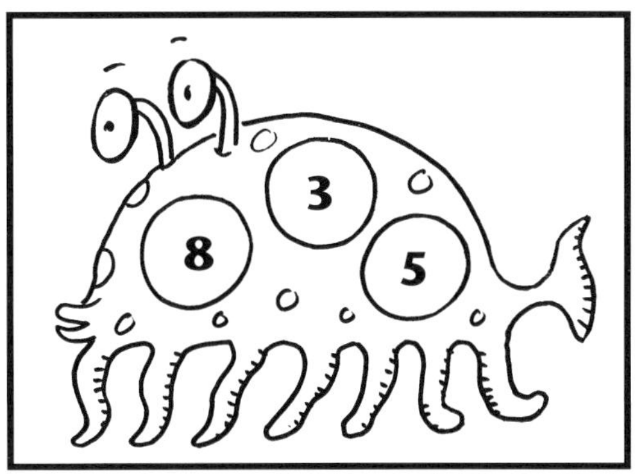

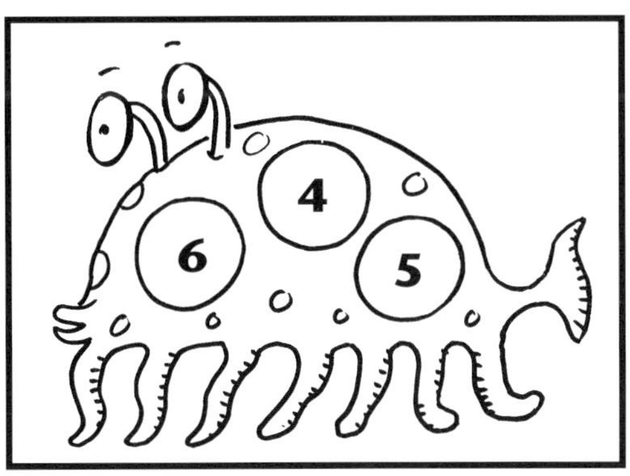

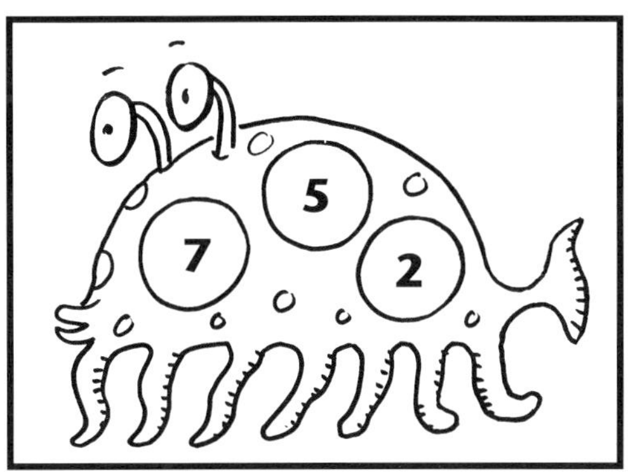

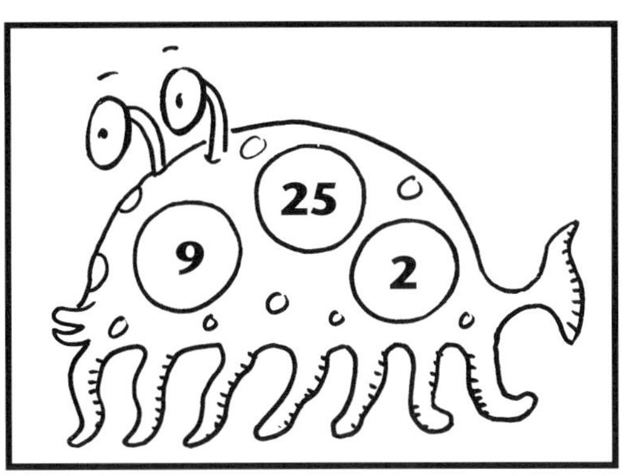

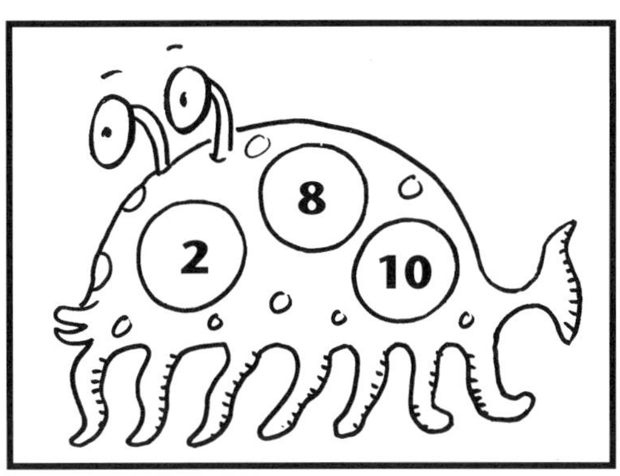

Easy peasy

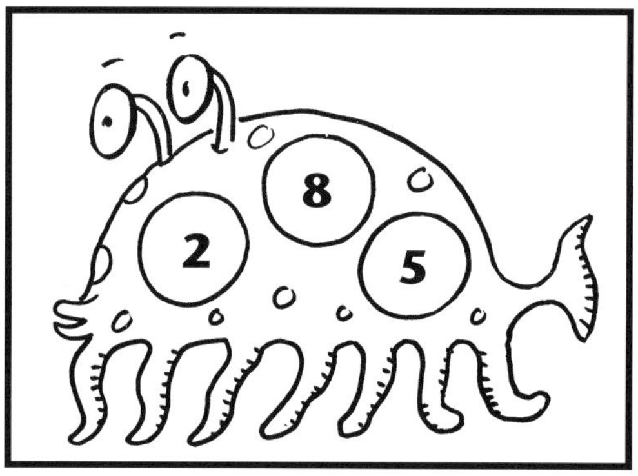

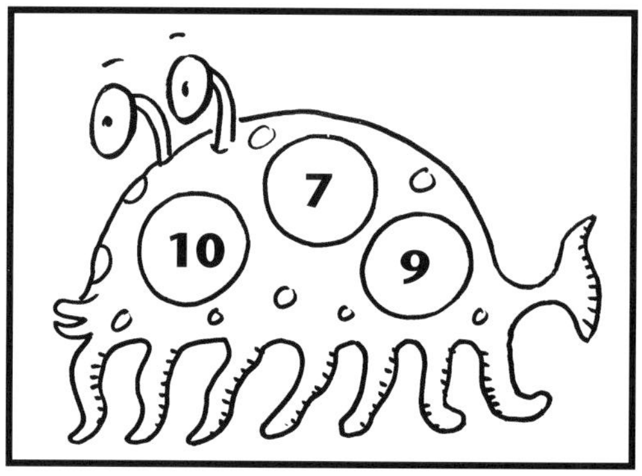

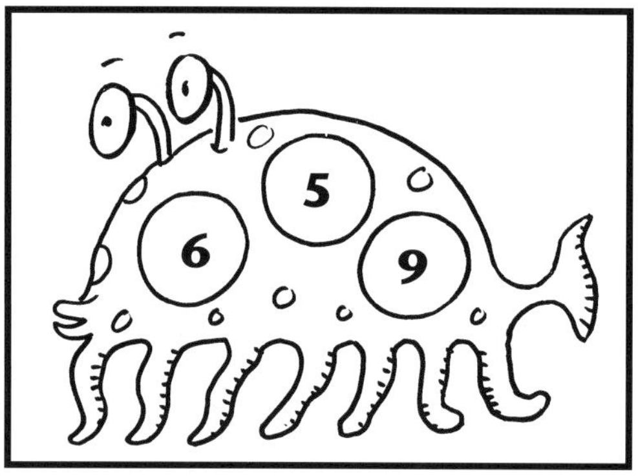

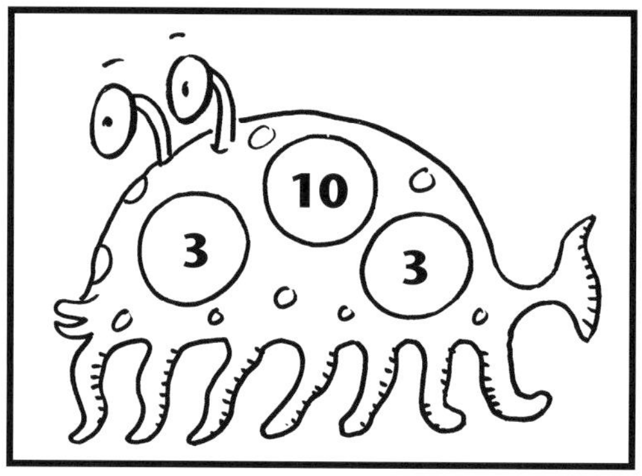

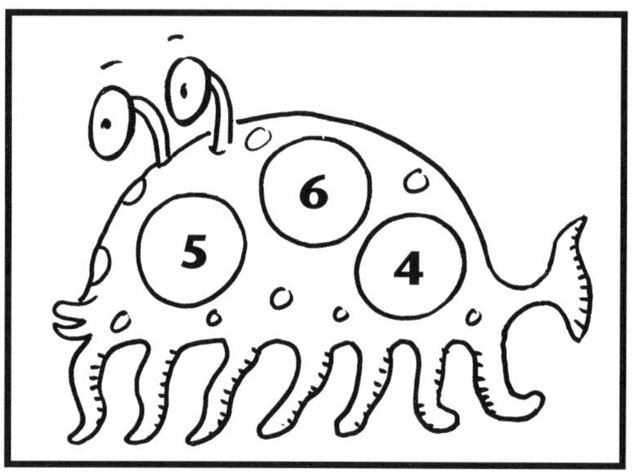

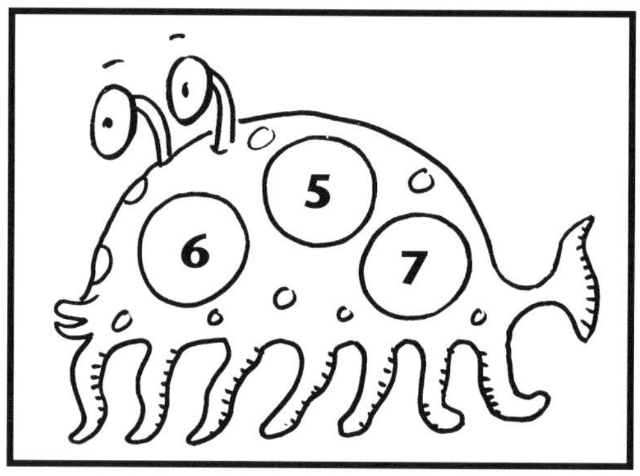

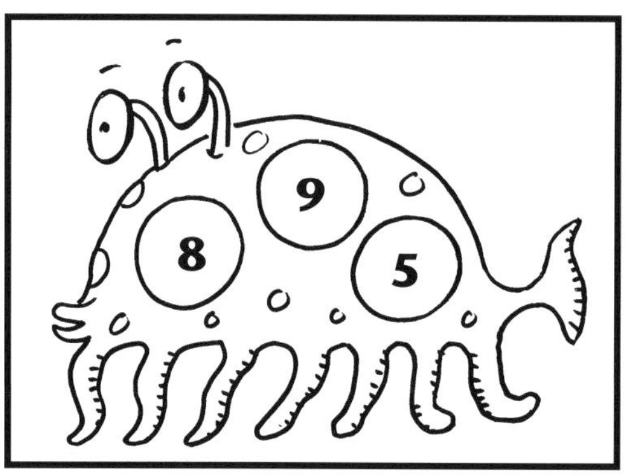

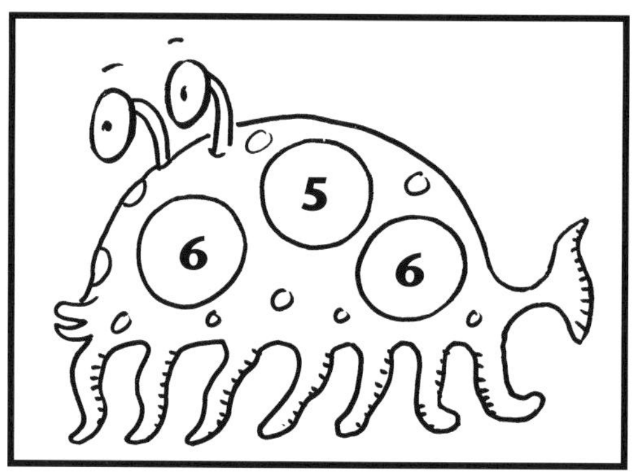

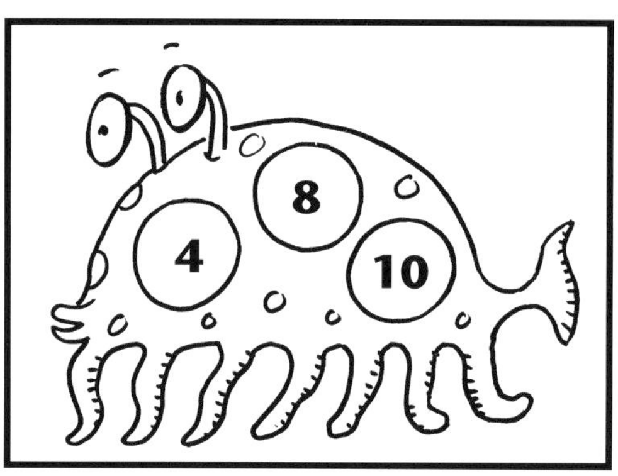

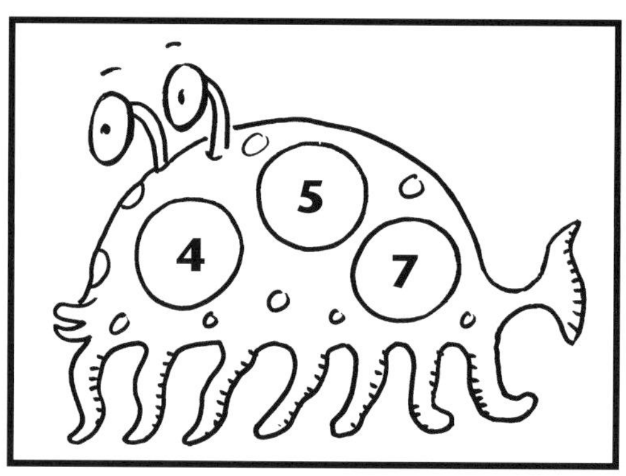

Easy peasy

$\square \times \square = \square$

$\square \times \square = \square$

$\square \times \square = \square$

$\square \times \square = \square$

Monster snap

Monster snap

Multiplication race

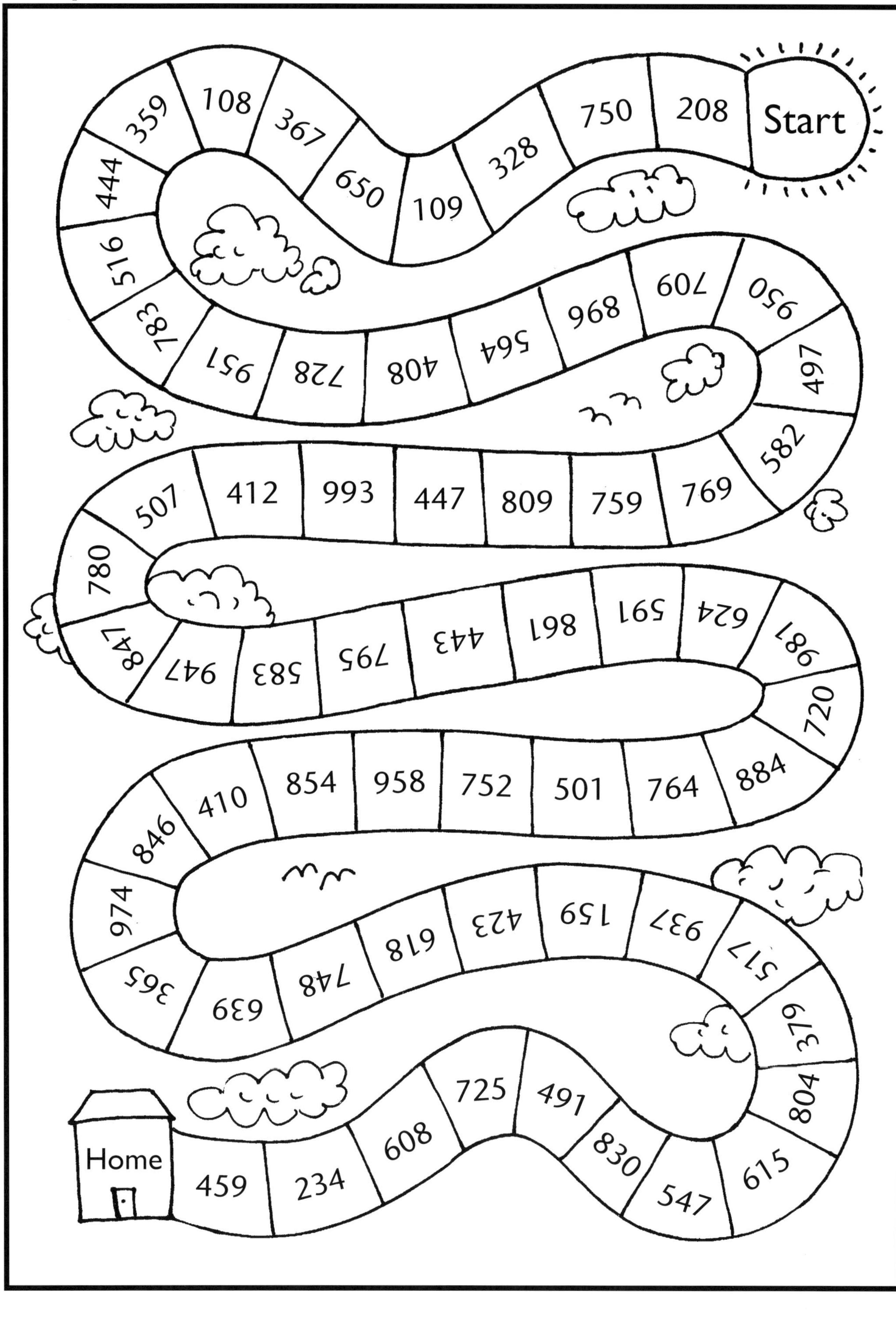

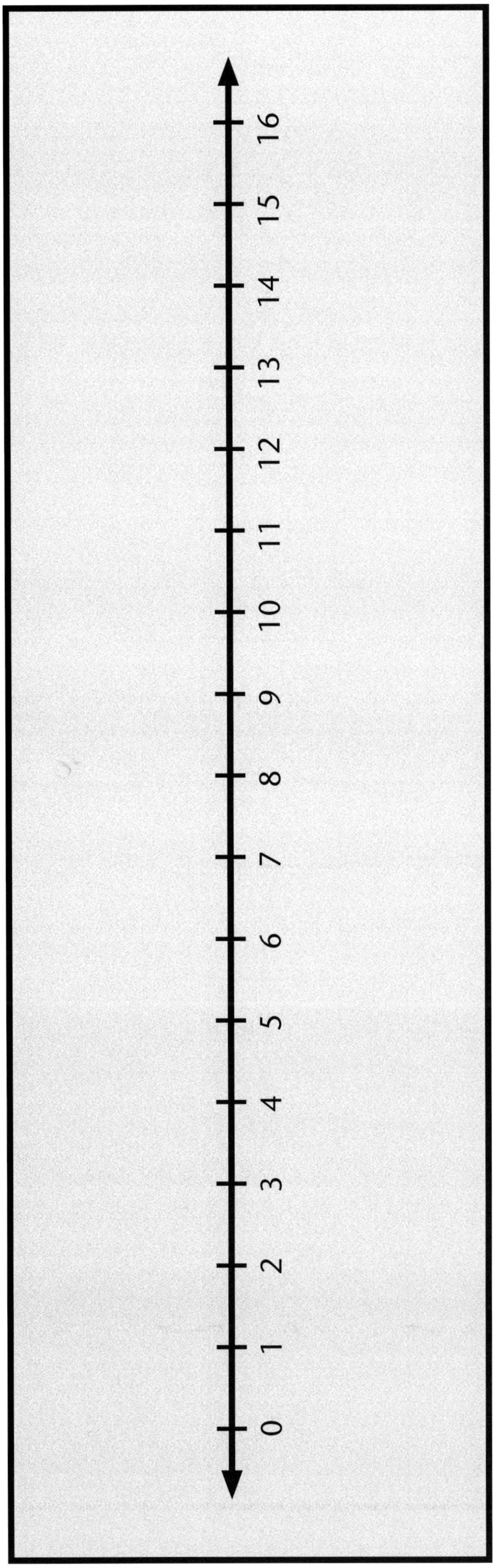
0
1
2
3
4
5
6
7
8
9
10
11
12
13
14
15
16

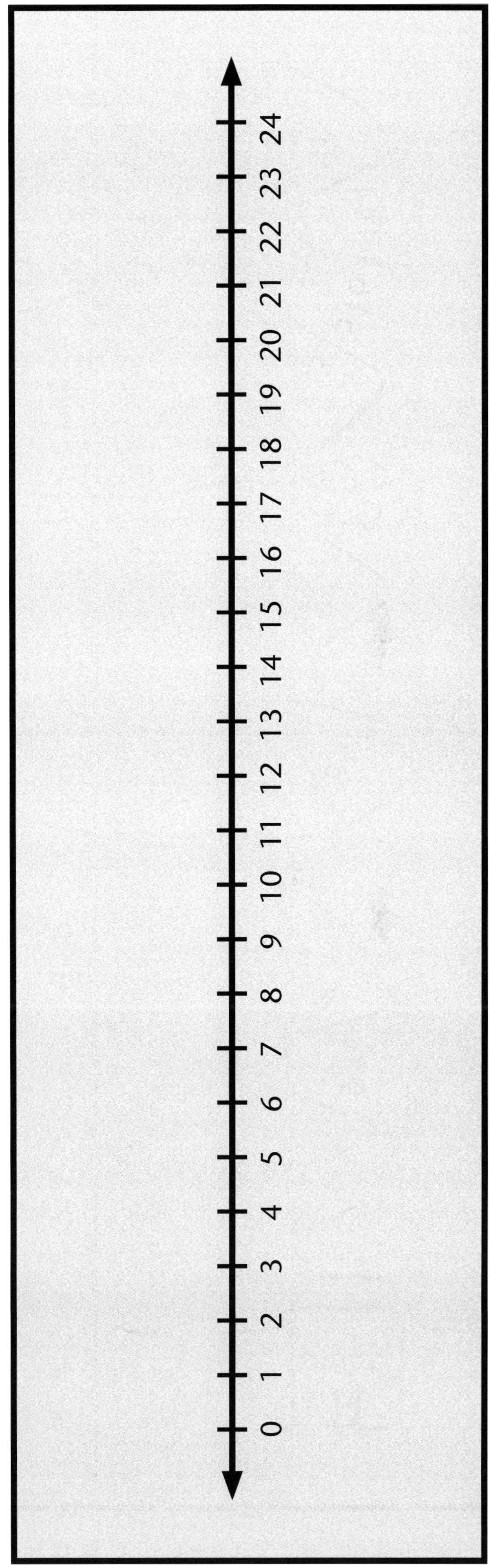
0
1
2
3
4
5
6
7
8
9
10
11
12
13
14
15
16
17
18
19
20
21
22
23
24

Get in line

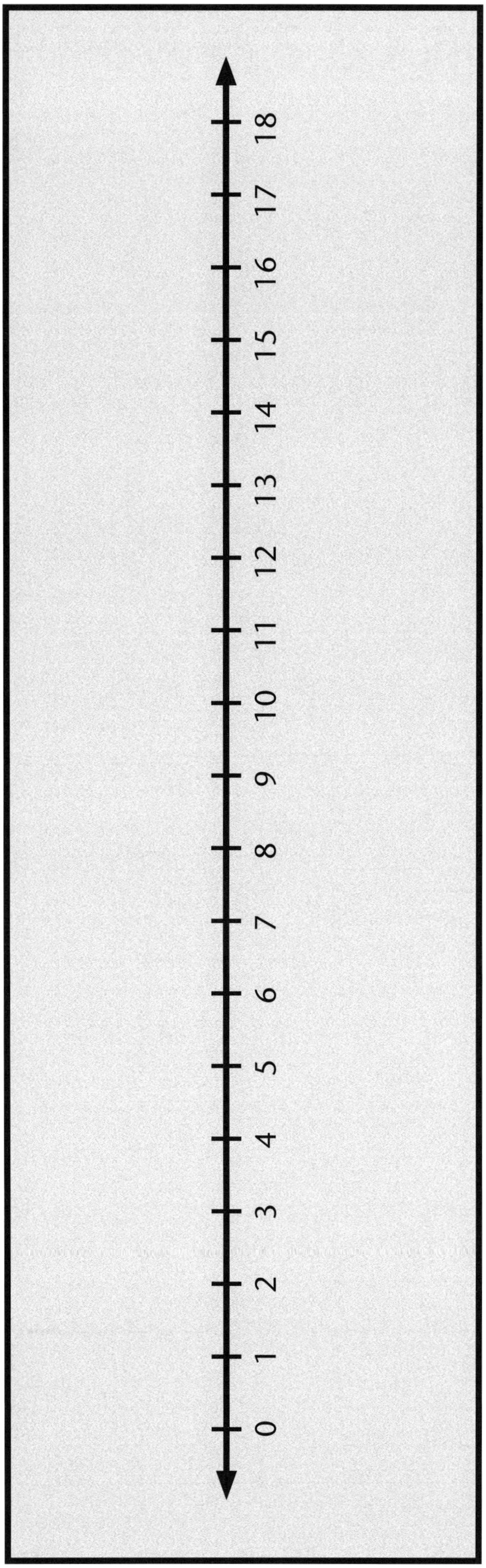
0
1
2
3
4
5
6
7
8
9
10
11
12
13
14
15
16
17
18

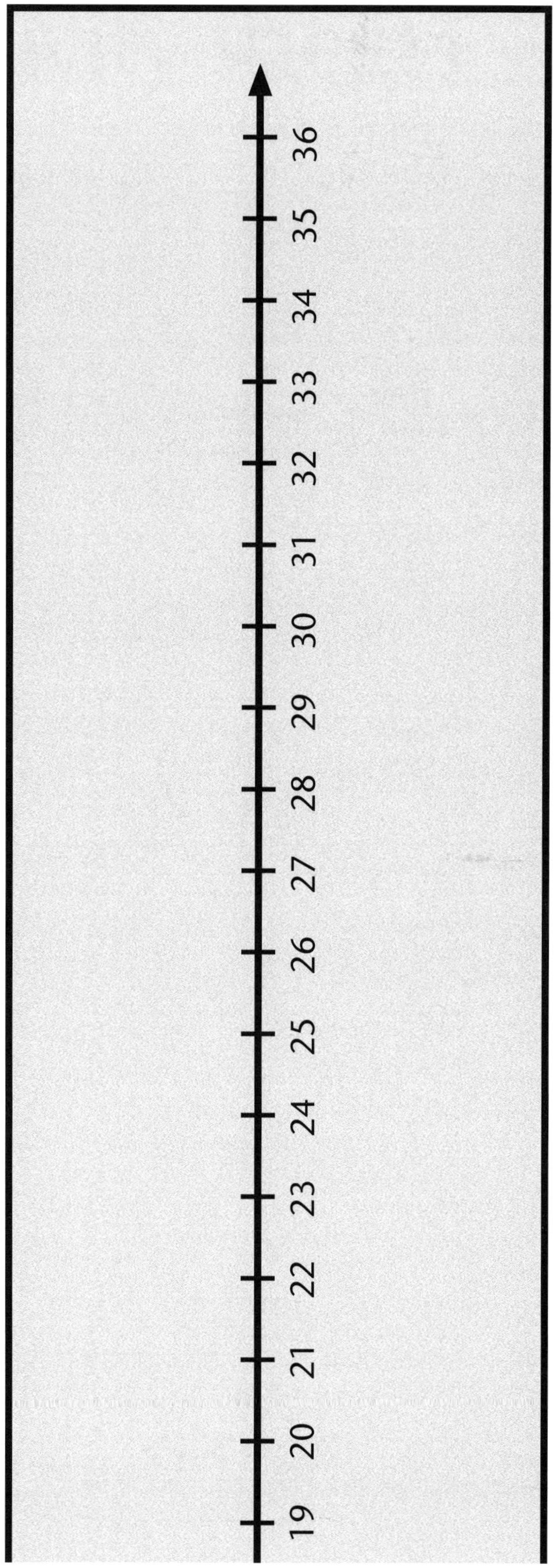
19
20
21
22
23
24
25
26
27
28
29
30
31
32
33
34
35
36

$16 \div 2 = \square$	$24 \div 3 = \square$
$16 \div 4 = \square$	$24 \div 6 = \square$
$16 \div 8 = \square$	$24 \div 8 = \square$
$18 \div 2 = \square$	$36 \div 2 = \square$
$18 \div 3 = \square$	$36 \div 3 = \square$
$18 \div 6 = \square$	$36 \div 4 = \square$
$18 \div 9 = \square$	$36 \div 6 = \square$
$24 \div 2 = \square$	$36 \div 9 = \square$

Fishy insides

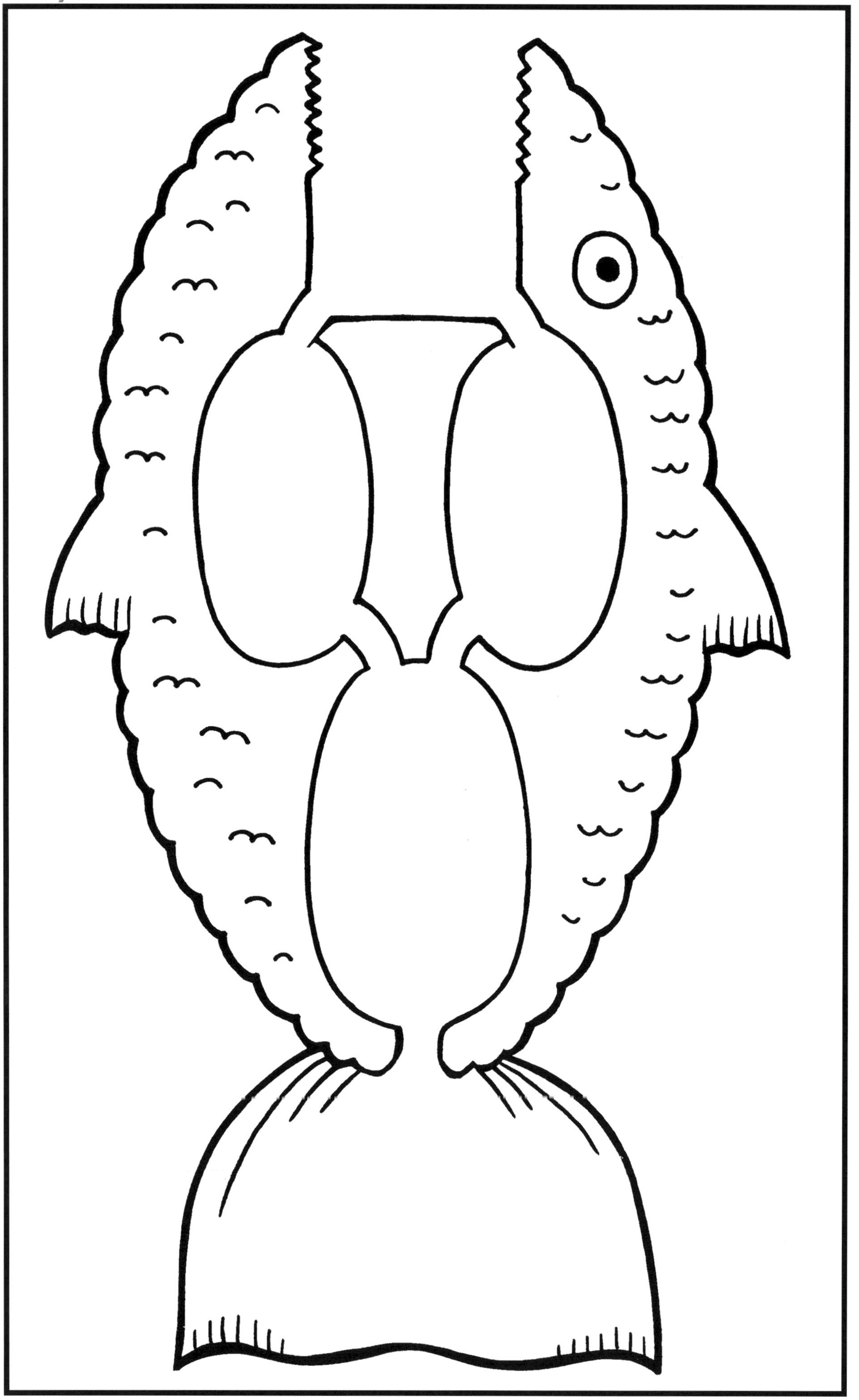

6×6	7×6	8×6
9×6	11×6	12×6
13×6	14×6	15×6
20×6	25×6	30×6
6×7	7×7	8×7
9×7	11×7	12×7

13 × 7	14 × 7	15 × 7
20 × 7	25 × 7	30 × 7
6 × 8	7 × 8	8 × 8
9 × 8	11 × 8	12 × 8
13 × 8	14 × 8	15 × 8
20 × 8	25 × 8	30 × 8

30	16
36	12

24	12
30	18

36	20
40	16

$10 \times 3 = \square$	$5 \times 6 = \square$
$2 \times 12 = \square$	$6 \times 4 = \square$
$3 \times 8 = \square$	$3 \times 6 = \square$
$2 \times 9 = \square$	$2 \times 8 = \square$
$16 \times 1 = \square$	$4 \times 4 = \square$
$6 \times 6 = \square$	$9 \times 4 = \square$
$2 \times 6 = \square$	$3 \times 4 = \square$
$4 \times 10 = \square$	$5 \times 8 = \square$

Links × and ÷ 3

☆ 27 ÷ 3	9 5 × 3
15 7 × 3	21 9 ÷ 3
3 24 ÷ 3	8 10 × 3
30 3 ÷ 3	1 6 × 3
18 6 ÷ 3	2 9 × 3
27 4 × 3	12 21 ÷ 3
7 15 ÷ 3	5 2 × 3
6 12 ÷ 3	4 30 ÷ 3
10 8 × 3	24 ★

☆	2×4	8	$16 \div 4$
4	6×4	24	9×4
36	$8 \div 4$	2	$28 \div 4$
7	4×4	16	10×4
40	$4 \div 4$	1	$24 \div 4$
6	8×4	32	$12 \div 4$
3	8×4	32	$20 \div 4$
5	7×4	28	$40 \div 4$
10	5×4	20	$36 \div 4$
9	3×4	12	★

Links × and ÷ 5

	25 ÷ 5	5	9 × 5
45	7 × 5	35	10 ÷ 5
2	50 ÷ 5	10	4 × 5
20	8 × 5	40	15 ÷ 5
3	6 × 5	30	45 ÷ 5
9	30 ÷ 5	6	2 × 5
10	5 ÷ 5	1	35 ÷ 5
7	3 × 5	15	5 × 5
25	40 ÷ 5	8	10 × 5
50	20 ÷ 5	4	

☆	36 ÷ 6	6	7 × 6
42	18 ÷ 6	3	30 ÷ 6
5	4 × 6	24	54 ÷ 6
9	8 × 6	48	10 × 6
60	12 ÷ 6	2	42 ÷ 6
7	2 × 6	12	24 ÷ 6
4	6 ÷ 6	1	60 ÷ 6
10	3 × 6	18	6 × 6
36	9 × 6	54	48 ÷ 6
8	5 × 6	30	★

☆	3×7	21	$14 \div 7$
2	$56 \div 7$	8	10×7
70	4×7	28	$49 \div 7$
7	2×7	14	$63 \div 7$
9	5×7	35	$21 \div 7$
3	8×7	56	$35 \div 7$
5	7×7	49	$28 \div 7$
4	6×7	42	$7 \div 7$
1	9×7	63	$42 \div 7$
6	$70 \div 7$	10	★

	9×8
48	$24 \div 8$
10	$16 \div 8$
56	3×8
5	$64 \div 8$
1	4×8
80	$56 \div 8$
16	8×8
6	$72 \div 8$
40	$32 \div 8$

72	6×8
3	$80 \div 8$
2	7×8
24	$40 \div 8$
8	$8 \div 8$
32	10×8
7	2×8
64	$48 \div 8$
9	5×8
4	

	4×9
1	7×9
3	10×9
2	2×9
5	$81 \div 9$
81	$36 \div 9$
8	6×9
10	5×9
6	8×9
27	$63 \div 9$
36	$9 \div 9$
63	$27 \div 9$
90	$18 \div 9$
18	$45 \div 9$
9	9×9
4	$72 \div 9$
54	$90 \div 9$
45	$54 \div 9$
72	3×9
7	

	300	10 × 30	700
70 × 10	500	50 × 10	650
65 × 10	900	30 × 30	350
70 × 5	1,200	60 × 20	540
54 × 10	8,600	860 × 10	5,400
60 × 90	720	80 × 90	360
40 × 9	1,800	20 × 90	250
5 × 50	490	7 × 70	1,000
20 × 50	810	90 × 9	250
25 × 10	3,200	40 × 80	

Shady problems

Answers to activity sheets

Page 5

A1.	674	4.	38
2.	4,567	5.	496
3.	28	6.	500
4.	6,432	7.	628
5.	597	8.	790
6.	98	9.	84
B1.	45	10.	1,604
2.	12	11.	725
3.	7	12.	3,518

Page 6

1.	£1,055	6.	£7,627
2.	£3,676	7.	£1,375
3.	£4,556	8.	£10,621
4.	£2,226	9.	£2,723
5.	£23,198	10.	£1,776

Page 7

1.	£1,476	£1,456
2.	£736	£726
3.	£5 015	£5,745
4.	£5,443	£5,453
5.	£816	£796
6.	£2,778	£2,408
7.	£1,007	£1,145

Page 8

1.	150	145	155
2.	240	234	246
3.	240	232	248
4.	800	796	804
5.	450	445	455
6.	6,400	6,392	6,408
7.	490	476	504
8.	2,700	2,691	2,709
9.	200	192	208
10.	2,100	2,097	2,103

Page 9

1.	200	195	205
2.	360	354	366
3.	400	392	408
4.	2,400	2,396	2,404
5.	400	395	405
6.	5,600	5,592	5,608
7.	630	616	644
8.	5,400	5,391	5,409
9.	280	272	288
10.	2,700	2,697	2,703

Page 10

1.	637	364	546	819
2.	245	392	343	196
3.	93	155	62	279
4.	552	138	414	276
5.	147	126	189	63

Page 11

1.	1,980	162	1,710	189
2.	1,860	294	3,060	168
3.	4,160	552	3,120	464
4.	1,640	236	1,280	272
5.	2,030	266	3,360	294

Page 12

1.	95	4.	128	7.	294
2.	126	5.	413	8.	474
3.	198	6.	118	9.	95

Page 13

1.	77	4.	186	7.	154
2.	99	5.	171	8.	198
3.	217	6.	133	9.	87

Page 14

1.	232	4.	126	7.	228
2.	114	5.	434		
3.	1,584	6.	87		

Page 15

1.	7	4.	7	7.	18
2.	7	5.	9		
3.	4	6.	9		

Page 16

1.	7	4.	20p	7.	4
2.	9	5.	8		
3.	6	6.	18p		

Page 17

1.	6	4.	9	7.	14
2.	9	5.	7		
3.	9	6.	8		

Page 18

1.	18	4.	27	7.	27
2.	42	5.	80		
3.	224	6.	343		

Page 19

1.	72	4.	8
2.	8	5.	17
3.	56	6.	5

Page 20

1.	16	32	6.	12	24
2.	18	36	7.	20	40
3.	16	32	8.	10	20
4.	12	24	9.	14	28
5.	28	56	10.	50	100

Page 21

1.	15	30	6.	27	54
2.	24	48	7.	12	24
3.	18	36	8.	21	42
4.	6	12	9.	9	18
5.	24	48	10.	32	64

Page 22

1.	6	3.	7	5.	4
2.	6	4.	4	6.	9

Page 23

1.	5	3.	6	5.	7
2.	3	4.	4	6.	8

Page 24

A1.	iii e 7	5.	i c 35
2.	iv b 4	B1.	6
3.	v a 63	2.	4
4.	ii d 9	3.	6

Page 25

A1.	ii c 9	5.	iv b 6
2.	v a 3	B1.	4
3.	i e 8	2.	9
4.	iii d 18	3.	16

Page 26

1.	£784	3.	£1,560
2.	£2,780	4.	£1,152

Page 27

1.	£12	3.	£20
2.	£14		£140
	£112		

Page 28

1.	Class 1 £58	2.	No
	Class 2 £70		Still to raise
	Class 3 £38		£120
	Class 4 £42		
	Profit £184		
	Still to raise		
	£166		

Page 29

1.	174	3.	£25
	232		£300
2.	£18		